Dare to Dream

Angela Dare

BookLeaf Publishing

Presentation by *BookLeaf Publishing*

Web: www.bookleafpub.com

E-mail: info@bookleafpub.com

ISBN: 9789357745802

First edition 2023

ACKNOWLEDGEMENT

I have to acknowledge Lawrence Maultsby for rekindling my interest in poetry and writing. He has motivated me to write when the words come to me. Such an inspiration to me.

Sunbeam

Sunbeams shine upon the waves
It is the beginning of a brand new day
The sun begins to rise from a deep deep sleep
The moon has gone to bed
Time for her to rest her weary head
Light will shine on
And make its way across the land
For a new day has dawn
Time for renewal
Time to recharge
A day to reflect
And time to push on

Grain of Sand

Each piece as intricate and delicate as a flower yet strong as a diamond. Thousand years of remodel and tore apart by storms of great magnitude to become the most beautiful art form

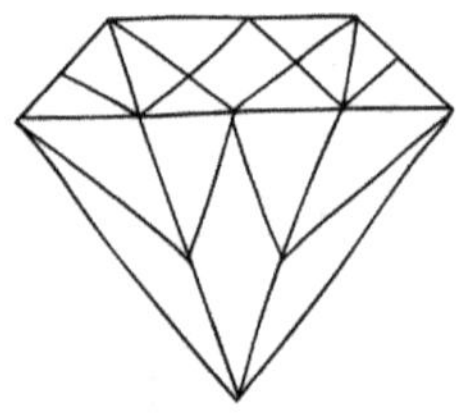

The Bounty

Dressed in my finest dress
Of deep dark purple and satin and lace
I meet my dark and handsome pirate
He is waiting on the gallows of the ship
Overlooking the calm moon-lit sea
His eyes turn my way
As the boat begins to sway
I try not to look away
The magic Stare is beyond compare
Seeking his gaze
We lock eyes
I move over to him
The moon shining so brightly
Not ever dim
We embrace in a dance
Upon the rocking of the waves
A quick kiss of the lips
Passionate embrace
We have intertwined in a way
That lovers cannot escape
It is a night for romance
As we plunder and play
Among the dancing waves

Loving you

You are my moon, stars and sun
You brighten my day
And keep the rain away
My love for you shall never fade
The dark days and cold nights are warmed by
your charm
Your touch, your kiss, your passion
It creates a spark that turns into flame
Two heartbeats become one
Together we will bond for eternity

Wonderful story

Luna sat in her lonely patch among the stars
Whispered to those near and far
No one could hear her faint echos
So she shown her light ever so bright
She gathered all the stars and made them twinkle
Planets played too and wanted to mingle
Light refracted off every shingle
Diamonds arose from the depths of the sea
Light shown down upon the land
Landed on you and me
Lit up our night
Made it heavenly
A passionate kiss
Love in full glory
This is just the beginning of a wonderful story

Destiny

There are times in life when you don't know
what is wrong and what is right
Only fate will decide our plight
Our life is one created by the universe
Our decisions have been set
It is up to us to follow them
Puzzle pieces shall fit
Piece by piece, make sure to never quit
Once the puzzle is complete
You have reached your final beautiful destiny

Writing is an art

Writing is an art
Can be simple, rhythmic, smart
Doesn't matter the topic
Life can be very myopic
List the words down
Let others figure it out
What we say is true
When the words flow in any tune

Words flow

Write about love
Write about fear
Write about anger
Write with hunger
Write with tears
Let the words flow
Who knows what will be tomorrow
Time waits for none
Will be beautiful once done

Love is the cure

Love is not forced
Love is not rushed
Love from the heart
Love from the soul
Love is pure
Love like no other
Love can be the cure

Raven and the moon

The raven perched upon the moon
Said to her
I am tired
I have lost my way among the clouds
Can I sit for a bit and rest my weariness
Oh but home is where I need to be
Oh beautiful moon
Please show me the way
Will you shine your light
So I may see the path that is in front of me
And the moon did just that
Shown her beautiful light to help guide the way

End of the day

The end of the day has come
Nightfall has begun
Time to drift off
Dreamland here we come
Let's meet there
In a field of dreams
The purest of love
We shall dance and sing
Until morning comes
And the night shall fade
We shall wake to embrace a brand new day

Love is sultry

Her hair made of silk
Lips sweet as milk
Neck so divine
Nipples like the finest wine
Honey spot so delicate
Taste of a flower
Hint of lavender
Sweet and tender
Souls are captured
They become one
Heartbeats run faster
Pressure no longer bound
Ultimate escape of pleasure
Paradise found

Tree Frog

Little tree frog
Tiny feet all webbed around
Holding you tightly bound
Onto the little limb that you have found
Soft rain falls
You still remain
Soaking up drops that cascade
Upon your small facade
You stay perched all day
Until the evening comes
It is now time to explore and play

Stranded

Day after day the loneliness creeps
Me questioning whether I want to live anymore
as I reach for an almost empty coconut to
quench my soul
I am slowly dying
This I just know
Will I ever leave this forsaken place where the
tides ebb and flow?
I watch the sea in hopes of a miracle
On the horizon I see something
it comes toward me slowly
I can see a flock of sea Turtles
they are escorting a woman
I rub my eyes in disbelief, how can this be? Who
is she?
She is dressed in a gown of shells
she has something for me
Her beauty I cannot comprehend
She sits beside me and hands me a coconut with
a liquid that is sure to quench my thirsty soul
So refreshing as I slowly sip the wonderful
concoction
She wipes my hair from my face and eyes and
looks deep down inside my tired soul

Slowly she places a kiss upon my forehead and
whispers sweet nothings in my ear
I take her hand in mine and tilt her face toward
me
Her eyes are like magic and fuels a fire filled
with passion
I lean in and kiss her and hold her
Sweet embrace
I feel saved
She has rescued me from my ultimate doom

Take a child fishing

Take a child fishing they say, hah,
Oh there has to be an easier way
The slippery worm
The bent hooks
The tangled lines
The fight, the struggle, oh, it is real
But to see a child smile
As a fish grabs the line
And fights it to eternity
It was worth it all the while

Dear child

My dear child
It is nearly time for you to fly
Fly away to another place
To a new time and space
For you must grow
And be able to sow
The seeds of love
Plant them in the deepest soil
And watch them multiply
Right before our very eyes
A love shall grow
It will overtake all
Nothing shall make it fall
Water it well with care
And the love shall prevail

Lasso the moon

Tie a lasso around the moon
Pull it down
Don't be shy
Hold on tight
it moves quickly
Adventure awaits
In space
As we sail among the stars

Poetry in the park

Sitting in the park
Reciting poetry
Thinking of words
That rhyme
Not caring much about the time
The beauty of it all
How sensual it is
Listening to poetry
Read to you
By the love of your life
Such grand delight
There is nothing that can compare.

Beauty from the stars

Love comes from the stars
Lands in your lap like an alien from Mars
But this one is from Venus
And has all the uniqueness
A beauty sent from the Heavens above

Wildflowers

Take me to where the wildflowers bloom
That is where my love will come true
Among the beauty and wilderness
Colors of the finest hues
It is here I will handpick one just for you
To show you that love can be wild, amazing and
true
A simple flower is all we need to fulfill our true
destiny

Sea in my veins

The love of the sea
It is in my veins
It is in my heart
It is deep within my soul
The salt air in my hair
The sand on my feet
The water lapping the shore
It is here I want to explore
Find plenty of shells galore
For this is my happy place
Among the dunes of the shore